Sea Turtles

written and photographed
by Frank Staub

HOUGHTON MIFFLIN

Boston • Atlanta • Dallas • Geneva, Illinois • Palo Alto • Princeton

For Dr. Shoop, Dr. Goertemiller, and the University of Rhode Island Department of Zoology

Thanks to our series consultant, Sharyn Fenwick, elementary science/math specialist. Mrs. Fenwick was the winner of the National Science Teachers Association 1991 Distinguished Teaching Award. She also was the recipient of the Presidential Award for Excellence in Math and Science Teaching, representing the state of Minnesota at the elementary level in 1992.

Special thanks to Dr. Jeanette Wyneken, Dr. Michael Salmon, and Dr. Ken Lohmann at Florida Atlantic University; Dr. C. Robert Shoop at University of Rhode Island; Dr. Lou Erhart at University of Central Florida; Carrie Keske-Crady at Florida Department of Environmental Protection; Richard Maretti and Tina Brown at The Sea Turtle Hospital; Miami Seaquarium; Marineland of Florida; and Aquarium of the Americas in New Orleans.

Photo on page 39 courtesy of Center for Marine Conservation

Sea Turtles by Frank Staub. Copyright © 1994 by Lerner Publications. Reprinted by arrangement with The Lerner Publishing Group. All rights reserved.

Houghton Mifflin Edition, 1999.

Printed in the U.S.A.

ISBN: 0-395-78121-3

3456789-WC-04 03 02 01 00 99 98

Contents

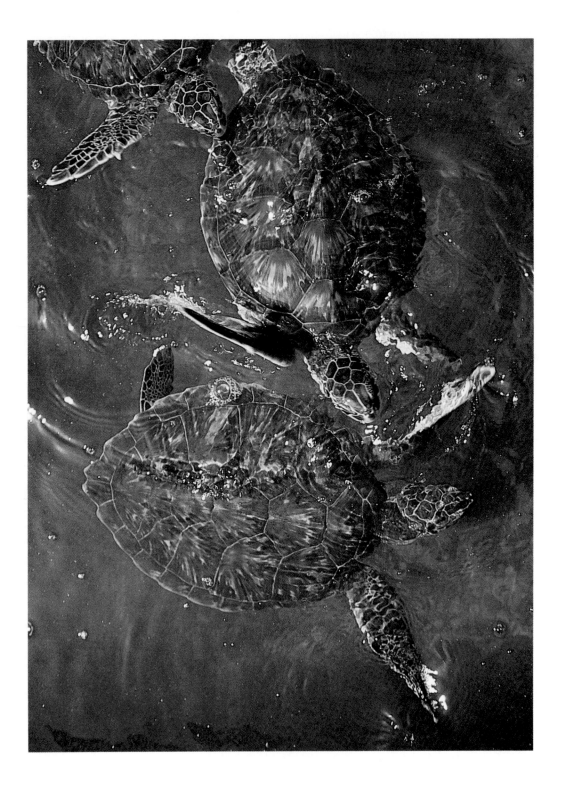

Alaska
(U.S.)

N

CANADA

UNITED STATES

MEXICO

Sea turtles spend most of their time in the ocean, but they come on land to lay their eggs. Some sea turtles lay their eggs in the United States. They lay their eggs somewhere along the coast that is highlighted in yellow.

Be a Word Detective

Can you find these words as you read about the sea turtle's life? Be a detective and try to figure out what they mean. You can turn to the glossary on page 47 for help.

flippers	**nesting**	**reptiles**
magnetic forces	**plankton**	**shell**
migrate		

Chapter 1

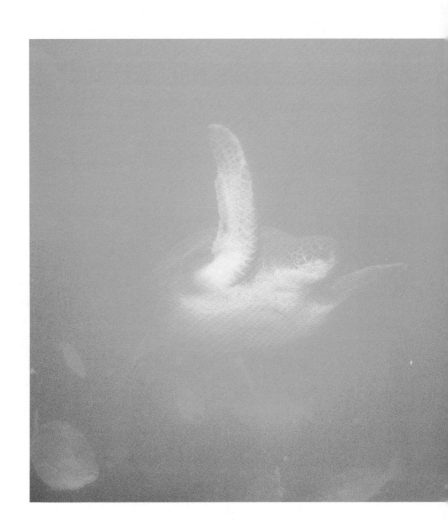

This is a green sea turtle. Do you think sea turtles are fast swimmers?

The Biggest Turtles

The world's biggest turtles don't walk on land. They swim in the sea. They are the sea turtles. Like most turtles, sea turtles hardly ever hurry. They usually swim slowly, flapping their great front flippers like birds in flight. But if they have to, sea turtles can swim fast. And they can swim very, very far.

This hawksbill sea turtle is flapping its front flippers to swim. Some sea turtles can swim up to 20 miles an hour.

All sea turtles, like the loggerhead turtle above and the green turtle below, must come to the water's surface to breathe air.

This old loggerhead turtle is resting under a ship's anchor.

Sea turtles spend most of their time under water. They can stay under water for about five or ten minutes. Then they have to come up for air. But if they don't swim around much, sea turtles can stay under water for hours. Divers sometimes find sea turtles sleeping under rocky ledges and sunken ships.

Like sea turtles, alligators are reptiles. Reptiles that spend a lot of time in water still must lay their eggs on land. This alligator is guarding her nest.

Sea turtles are reptiles. Snakes, lizards, and alligators are reptiles too. Reptiles have lungs to breathe air. Many reptiles eat, sleep, or travel in the water. But they still must come on land to lay their eggs.

Long ago, most turtles lived on land. These land turtles began to spend more and more time in the sea, or ocean. As thousands of years passed, the turtles' legs changed into flippers.

Their shells became flatter to make swimming easier. That happened about 150 million years ago. At that time, other reptiles called dinosaurs walked the earth. Then the environment changed, and all the dinosaurs died. But the sea turtles stayed safe in their watery home.

Sea turtles, like this male loggerhead, cannot pull their heads into their shells the way land turtles do.

Five main kinds of sea turtles live in the ocean waters of the United States. They are the leatherback, the loggerhead, the ridley, the hawksbill, and the green.

The hawksbill sea turtle's scientific name is
Eretmochelys imbricata.

The green sea turtle's scientific name is Chelonia mydas. *Green sea turtles are about 3 feet long and weigh about 300 pounds.*

Leatherbacks are the biggest reptiles alive today. They can grow as big as a bathtub. Most turtles have a hard shell. But the leatherback is covered by dark, leathery skin.

The ridley sea turtle in front has the scientific name of Lepidochelys kempi. *It will grow to be about 30 inches long and to weigh about 100 pounds. A loggerhead sea turtle is behind the ridley.*

The scientific name of the loggerhead sea turtle is Caretta caretta. *Loggerheads grow to be about 3 feet long and to weigh up to 350 pounds.*

All the other sea turtles have hard shells. Loggerheads have a big head and a long reddish shell, shaped like a heart. More loggerheads live in the United States than any other sea turtle. Ridleys are the smallest sea

We know less about the hawksbill than any other sea turtle.

turtles. They have a round shell about the size of a large pizza. Hawksbill turtles have a beak shaped like the beak of a hawk. Green turtles have green fat. All these different sea turtles live their lives in almost the same way.

Chapter 2

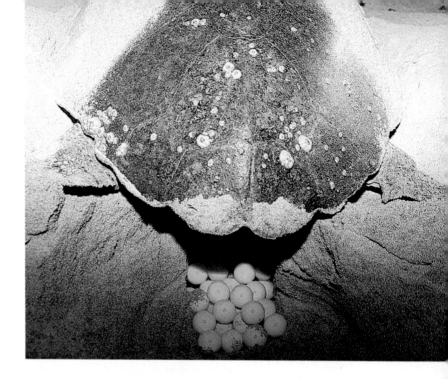

A female loggerhead sea turtle is laying her eggs on a beach at night. Do male sea turtles ever come on land?

Nests in the Sand

Most of a sea turtle's life is a mystery. It's hard for us to watch and learn about sea turtles in the water. Male sea turtles stay in the water and almost never come on land. But female sea turtles come on land to lay their eggs. They swim through crashing waves to drag their heavy bodies up onto a beach. This is the time we learn the most about sea turtles.

In the ocean, water holds up the big turtles. But on land, they can barely stand. A female sea turtle crawls up to where the sand is dry. Then she starts digging her nest. Digging a nest is hard work. First, she uses her front flippers to clear away the loose sand on the surface. Then she uses her rear flippers to dig a

Most sea turtles crawl out of the sea at night to lay their eggs.

deep hole for the eggs. If she hits a rock or a root, she may stop digging. She may also stop if a person comes near. Then she goes back to the sea.

Most sea turtles nest about six times in one year. But they may skip two to four years before they nest again.

A sea turtle's nest hole is about 20 inches deep.

After the sea turtle digs as deep as she can reach, she rests. Then she lays her eggs. The eggs come out one by one or two by two. Sea turtle eggs look like big Ping-Pong balls. The shells are soft and rubbery. Sometimes the eggs bounce as they fall.

Some scientists study sea turtles by counting their eggs.

A mother sea turtle lays about 100 eggs. She lays so many eggs because some of the babies won't hatch. Most of the baby turtles who do hatch die before they grow up.

After the last egg is laid, the mother turtle pushes sand back into the hole. Then she throws loose sand around so the nest is hard to see. Making a nest and laying eggs is called nesting. Nesting takes about an hour for loggerheads. But green turtles dig deeper nests. They may take many hours to nest.

Sea turtles are careful to hide their nests by covering them with sand.

As the sea turtle drags herself back down to the sea, she stops to rest often. But she doesn't look back. Now the sand is mother to her eggs.

The city lights could cause this nesting sea turtle to crawl the wrong way.

Raccoons love to eat eggs and baby sea turtles.

It protects them from the sun and heat. But raccoons, coyotes, foxes, wild dogs, ants, and even people may dig up the eggs and eat them. Also, heavy rains and big waves may flood the nest and kill the eggs.

This sea turtle isn't sad. She is just getting rid of salt through her tears.

While she is on land, you can see tears in the sea turtle's eyes. Some people think she is sad because she is leaving her eggs in the sand. But sea turtles don't cry because they are sad.

They cry to get rid of salt. The only water a sea turtle ever drinks is salty ocean water. All animals need some salt. But too much salt can make an animal sick. The extra salt in a sea turtle's body comes out in tears. We see the tears only when the turtle's face is dry.

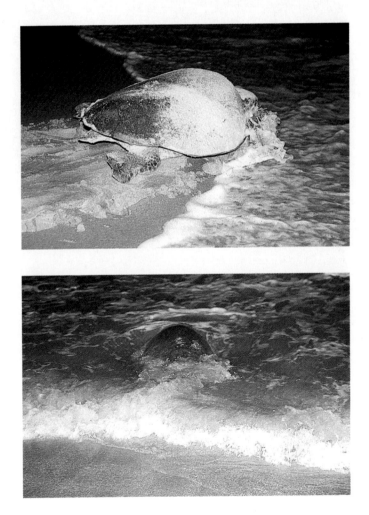

This loggerhead's job is done for now. In Florida, loggerheads nest from late April through September.

Chapter 3

Leatherback sea turtles have the scientific name of Dermochelys coriacea. *How big do you think this baby leatherback was when it hatched?*

Babies at Sea

Baby sea turtles hatch about two months after the eggs are laid. Each baby turtle is smaller than a bar of soap. As more and more babies hatch, they start moving their flippers. This makes the sand that's above the babies fall down below them. So sand in the ceiling of the nest becomes the sand on the floor. Slowly, the babies move upward. About three days after hatching, the babies are just below the sand's surface.

A baby loggerhead is hatching. Normally, baby sea turtles hatch in their sandy nests.

Once the little turtles are free of the sand, they must get to the water. But which way is that? They've never seen the ocean before. And they leave the nest only at night. But even on the darkest beaches, baby sea turtles see the

Some baby loggerheads are just coming out of their nest. They are only 2 inches long.

Only about 1 out of 1,000 baby sea turtles lives long enough to become an adult. These baby loggerheads were lucky to make it safely to the sea.

tall, black shadows of plants. They crawl away from these shadows and crawl toward the water. But sometimes the babies move toward the lights of a house or road. Baby sea turtles have crawled onto highways and even baseball fields.

Ghost crabs eat sea turtle eggs and baby sea turtles.

Even if a baby sea turtle goes the right way, it may not reach the water. Crabs and birds love to eat baby sea turtles. The baby's shell is soft and easy to bite into. If a baby sea turtle reaches the ocean, it keeps flapping its flippers. Now it must swim, for it faces another danger—hungry fishes.

Baby sea turtles swim all night long and all through the next day. They keep swimming until they are many miles from shore. Here they have few enemies. The water below them may be a mile deep. Their only food is tiny animals called plankton. Plankton float near the surface of the water. For the next year or so, the little sea turtles float in the sea, just like the plankton they eat.

Baby sea turtles, like this leatherback, swim until they are far away from land.

Chapter 4

When green sea turtles grow to be about 10 inches long, they swim closer to shore. What do you think they eat?

Life along the Coast

Baby sea turtles grow quickly if they find enough plankton to eat. After a few years, they reach the size of a dinner plate. Now they need food that is bigger than plankton. So most of the young turtles swim back to shallow water. Here they can munch on food from the sea floor. Green turtles graze on sea grasses.

Ridleys eat crabs. Hawksbills like sponges. Loggerheads eat many different kinds of animals. The leatherback stays out at sea, where it eats jellyfish.

Now the turtles' shells have grown hard. Most of the big fishes, who tried to eat them as babies, leave them alone. But sometimes, sharks attack even the biggest turtles. That's why so many sea turtles are missing pieces of their flippers and shells.

Although sharks eat sea turtles, this shark doesn't seem interested in eating the green turtle behind it.

Chapter 5

When it is nesting time, sea turtles probably swim back to where they hatched. Do they have to swim very far?

Long-Distance Travelers

No one knows how old sea turtles are when they nest for the first time. But we do know that sea turtles swim back to the area where they hatched. Some scientists think sea turtles lay their eggs on the same beaches used by their mothers, grandmothers, great-grandmothers, great-great-grandmothers, and so on. By the time they are ready to nest, sea turtles may be very far from their nesting beaches. So they have to migrate.

Loggerheads nest in Florida, but they look for food in the sea as far north as New Jersey, and as far south as the Dominican Republic.

When an animal migrates, it moves from one place to another place. Birds who fly south for the winter then north for the summer are migrating. Some sea turtles migrate thousands of miles. They travel between their nesting beaches and their feeding places.

How does a sea turtle know where to nest? And how does it find its way there, across so many miles of ocean? Maybe the sea turtles use

Some sea turtles travel thousands of miles to get to their nesting beaches.

This ridley sea turtle has a tag on its flipper so scientists can track how far it travels.

the sun and stars. Maybe they smell their way there, like a dog looking for its home. Or maybe they feel the earth in a very special way. The earth gives off little pushing and pulling forces, just like a giant magnet. We can't feel these forces, but sea turtles can. Feeling the earth's magnetic forces may help sea turtles find their way through the sea.

Chapter 6

An animal dug up this sea turtle nest and ate all the eggs. Do you think sea turtles face many other dangers?

Save the Sea Turtles

We still have a lot to learn about sea turtles. But we do know that there aren't as many sea turtles as there used to be. Sea turtles die when they eat plastic bags, tar, and other trash floating on the ocean. Sea turtles also die when they get tangled up in old fishing lines.

Some sea turtles get caught in fishing nets. They die too. Buildings now stand on many of the sea turtle's nesting beaches. So sea turtles have fewer places to lay their eggs than they used to.

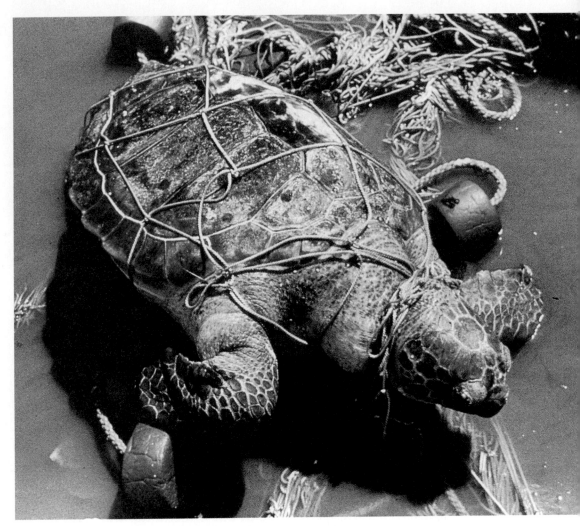

This loggerhead got tangled up in a fishing net and died.

This baby leatherback will grow to be about 8 feet long and weigh up to 2,000 pounds! Leatherbacks can be killed by eating plastic bags. Plastic bags look like their favorite food, jellyfish.

In some places, sea turtle nests are surrounded by cages to protect the eggs from raccoons, crabs, and people.

In some countries, people hunt sea turtles for their meat. They also make leather from the sea turtle's skin and jewelry from its shell. At one time, only a small number of people hunted sea turtles. They killed only what they needed for themselves. Then more and more sea turtles were caught for people in other countries. Now there aren't enough sea turtles to catch anymore.

Signs, like the one below, warn people about protecting sea turtles. The Sea Turtle Hospital helps keep sea turtles healthy. This green sea turtle has had a warty growth removed.

ATTENTION
BEACH
USERS
HELP PROTECT ENDANGERED SEA TURTLES
•AVOID DISTURBING NESTING FEMALES
•LEAVE NEST, EGGS AND HATCHLINGS UNDISTURBED
•TURN OFF LIGHTS THAT SHINE ON BEACH
(BETWEEN MAY 1ST OCT. 31ST)
SEA TURTLES ARE PROTECTED BY COUNTY STATE
AND FEDERAL LAW. FINES UP TO $20,000.
FOR MORE INFO. CONTACT 633-2016

Almost everyone cares about sea turtles and wants to save them. They are among nature's greatest wonders. They swim mile after mile across the deep sea. When it's time to nest, the females drag their huge bodies up onto the sand. They may nest on the same beach used by their families for hundreds, or maybe thousands, of years. And all they have to guide them is the water, the earth, and the sky.

The morning sun shines down on tracks made the night before by a nesting sea turtle.

On Sharing a Book

As you know, adults greatly influence a child's attitude toward reading. When a child sees you read, or when you share a book with a child, you're sending a message that reading is important. Show your child that reading a book together is important to you. Find a comfortable, quiet place. Turn off the television and limit other distractions like telephone calls.

Be prepared to start slowly. Take turns reading parts of this book. Stop and talk about what you're reading. Talk about the photographs. You may find that much of the shared time is spent discussing just a few pages. This discussion time is valuable for both of you, so don't move through the book too quickly. If your child begins to lose interest, stop reading. Continue sharing the book at another time. When you do pick up the book again, be sure to revisit the parts you have already read. Most importantly, enjoy the book!

Be a Vocabulary Detective

You will find a word list on page 5. Words selected for this list are important to the understanding of the topic of this book. Encourage your child to be a word detective and search for the words as you read the book together. Talk about what the words mean and how they are used in the sentence. Do any of these words have more than one meaning? You will find these words defined in a glossary on page 47.

What about Questions?

Use questions to make sure your child understands the information in this book. Here are some suggestions:

> What did this paragraph tell us? What does this picture show? What do you think we'll learn about next? Tell me about the sea turtle's life in the ocean. Tell me about the sea turtle's life on land. How is it like ours? How is it different? Could a sea turtle live in your backyard? Why/Why not? What would you need to live where sea turtles live? What do you think it's like living in the sea? What would happen if there were no sea turtles? What is your favorite part in the book?

If your child has questions, don't hesitate to respond with questions of your own like: What do *you* think? Why? What is it that you don't know? If your child can't remember certain facts, turn to the index.

Introducing the Index

The index is an important learning tool. It helps readers get information quickly without searching throughout the whole book. Turn to the index on page 48. Choose an entry, such as *flippers,* and ask your child to use the index to find out when sea turtles use their flippers. Repeat this exercise with as many entries as you like. Ask your child to point out the differences between an index and a glossary. (The glossary tells readers what words mean, while the index helps readers find information quickly.)

Where in the World?

Many plants and animals found in the Early Bird Nature Books series live in parts of the world other than the United States. Encourage your child to find the places mentioned in this book on a world map or globe. Take time to talk about climate, terrain, and how your family might live in such places.

All the World in Metric!

Although our monetary system is in metric units (based on multiples of 10), the United States is one of the few countries in the world that does not use the metric system of measurement. Here are some conversion activities you and your child can do using a calculator:

WHEN YOU KNOW:	MULTIPLY BY:	TO FIND:
miles	1.609	kilometers
feet	0.3048	meters
inches	2.54	centimeters
gallons	3.787	liters
tons	0.907	metric tons
pounds	0.454	kilograms

Family Activities

Imagine being a sea turtle on land. How would you move? How would you make your nest? Imagine being a baby sea turtle. Now how would you move?

Male sea turtles have much longer tails than female sea turtles. Look through the book and see if you can find any males.

Visit a zoo and find all the different types of reptiles. How are they the same? How are they different?

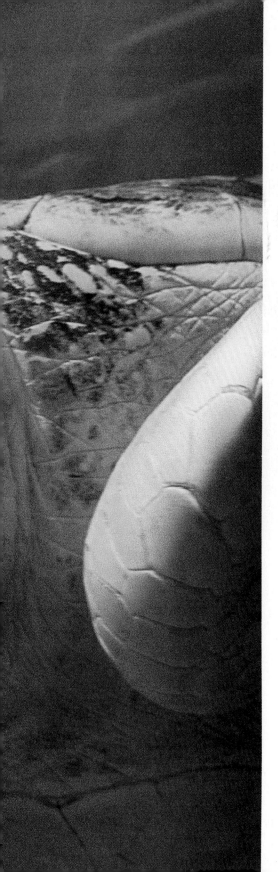

Glossary

flippers—wide, flat arms or legs specially made for swimming

magnetic forces—Pushing and pulling movements created by something in the earth. Magnetic forces may help sea turtles find their way from one place to another.

migrate—to travel back and forth between feeding places and nesting areas

nesting—making a nest and laying eggs

plankton—tiny animals and plants floating in the sea. Baby sea turtles eat plankton.

reptiles—a group of animals that includes turtles, snakes, lizards, crocodiles, and alligators

shell—the hard covering surrounding turtles and some other animals

Index